Sew Much Fun

14 Projects to Stitch & Machine Embroider

C&T PUBLISHING

© 2002 by Oklahoma Embroidery Supply & Design

Developmental Editors: Barb Kuhn, Carolyn Aune

Technical Editor: Carolyn Aune

Copy Editor: Lucy Grijalva

Cover Designer: Kristen Yenche

Book Designer: Kristen Yenche

Illustrator: Kirstie L. McCormick

Production Assistant: Kirstie L. McCormick

Photography: Christy Burcham/OESD, Kirstie L. McCormick/C&T Publishing

Published by C&T Publishing, Inc., P.O. Box 1456, Lafayette, California 94549

Front and Back Cover Photography: Kirstie L. McCormick

Attention Teachers: C&T Publishing, Inc. encourages you to use this book as a text for teaching. Contact us at 800-284-1114 or www.ctpub.com for more information about the C&T Teachers Program.

Library of Congress Cataloging-in-Publication Data

Sew much fun: 14 projects to stitch & embroider / Oklahoma Embroidery Supply & Design.

p. cm.

ISBN 1-57120-180-7

1. Embroidery, Machine--Patterns. I. Oklahoma Embroidery Supply & Design.

TT772 .S48 2002

746.44--dc21

2002005470

Printed in China

10 9 8 7 6 5 4 3 2 1

PREFACE

elcome! You are about to discover a whole new universe of creative stitchery…right in your own sewing room. All you need is a computerized sewing machine with embroidery capabilities, and you'll soon be stitching a wide variety of fast, fun, and easy projects for yourself, your home, and everyone in your family---even the kids! And, because these projects work up so quickly, and are created from a variety of simple make-it-yourself or readily available pre-made items, they make ideal gifts for housewarmings, bridal showers, anniversaries, and birthdays as well.

Projects range from quilts to home accessories, each embellished with delightful machine-embroidered motifs. Step-by-step instructions--with photos--walk you smoothly through each project. The accompanying CD includes all of the embroidery designs you see in the book, and complete resource catalogs for both Oklahoma Embroidery Supply and Design and C & T Publishing. As an added bonus, we've included Magic Sizing software that allows you to "play" with options beyond those included in these pages.

Just a note: The basic embroidery instructions in Sew Much Fun are not specific to one particular make or model of sewing machine. They are geared specifically for the projects in this book, and are not intended as a comprehensive course in basic machine embroidery technique. If you are unfamiliar with the elementary "how-tos" or the capabilities of your particular machine, we suggest that you consult the machine's manual. Better yet, contact the shop or dealer from whom you purchased the machine. These helpful folks often provide excellent intro-ductory classes as part of their service.

TABLE OF

EMBROIDERY PROJECTS

Family Room Favorites

CONTENTS

EMBROIDERY BASICS

When you machine embroider, several major factors influence the quality of the finished design: they include embroidery machine (or module) maintenance, the embroidery design itself, the products used, and the user technique.

EMBROIDERY MACHINE MAINTENANCE

Once a year, take your machine to a qualified technician for a tune-up. Regular maintenance keeps your machine running smoothly and prevents future problems.

The home machines on the market today produce high-quality embroidery. However, if a machine is not properly maintained, the quality of the embroidery suffers. When you embroider, your machine works harder than when you do regular sewing. You'll need to maintain your machine accordingly. Clean and oil your machine following the manufacturer's instructions.

QUALITY OF THE EMBROIDERY DESIGN

There is no rule that says your sample must be sewn on white fabric. Be creative! The test design can be made into a patch, quilt square, sachet, or added to another small project.

Not all designs are created equal! For best results, choose professionally created designs. Test the design before using it on a project. Use the same thread, needle, fabric, and stabilizer as used in the project itself. Making a test design is well worth the time and expense. It is much less expensive to test the design than to replace a ruined project.

EMBROIDERY PRODUCTS

As the "hobby" of home embroidery has expanded to include more and more crafters, so has the availability of high-quality embroidery supplies. Long gone are the days when embroiderers had to make do with supplies not intended for embroidery (such as using interfacing as embroidery stabilizer). While there are many specialty and novelty items available to make embroidery easy and fun, the embroiderer needs only four categories of supplies on an ongoing basis. These are thread, fabric, needles, and stabilizer.

Thread:

Many types of embroidery threads are available. Here are some to try:

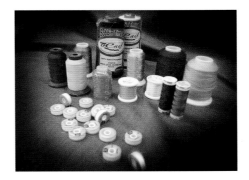

- *Polyester thread* has a high sheen and a high tensile strength, which results in fewer thread breaks. Polyester thread is also UV resistant, colorfast, and heat resistant.

- *Rayon thread* is commonly used because of its high sheen. It is not heat resistant or colorfast (it may bleed onto a garment or accept color from the garment). Take care when laundering the embroidered garment.

- *Cotton thread* is used when a flat finish is desired. It has a low tensile strength so it breaks easily.

- *Bobbin thread* for embroidery is a special lightweight thread used in the bobbin in order to keep the thread from building up on the underneath side of the design, which can cause stitching problems.

For thread sizes, the larger the number, the smaller the thread.

Fabric:

Fabric type is not an issue when selecting designs to use on a project. There are very few fabrics that cannot be embroidered. However, you do need to consider the fabric strength when choosing the embroidery design. A lightweight tulle or batiste needs an airy, light design. Heavier fabrics such as denim can tolerate more densely stitched designs.

Needles:

- Needles designated for embroidery are best. These typically have a larger eye to allow the specialty thread to pass through without breaking.

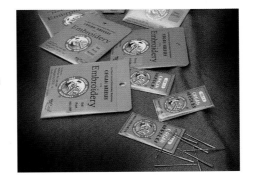

Needles come with a variety of points, each appropriate for a different type of fabric.

Sharps, which pierce the fibers of the fabric, are used for woven fabrics.

Ballpoints are used for knits because they will not break the fibers.

Universal points can be used for either woven fabrics or knits.

Wedge points are used for sewing leather because they have a sword-like point that cuts a small hole in the leather for the thread to pass through.

We recommend that you replace the needle after five hours of stitching embroidery. This can be anywhere from three large to twenty small embroidery designs. If in doubt about whether to change the needle, go ahead and change it.

For needle sizes, the larger the number, the larger the size of the needle.

The more stitches the design has, the heavier the stabilizer you will need. If you only have a lightweight stabilizer, use several layers of stabilizer. Four is not too many. Sometimes multiple layers of stabilizer are better than using one layer of heavier stabilizer.

■ Changing the Needle: As in regular sewing, it is important to replace needles often. Embroidering with a dull needle can cause skipped or irregular stitches. Worse, the needle could break and ruin the embroidery or damage the fabric.

■ Needles come in a variety of sizes. The standard size for embroidery is 80/12, which can be used on most medium-weight fabrics. Finer fabrics, such as satins, need a smaller needle, such as a 70/10 or a 75/11. Heavier fabrics like denim need a 90/14 or larger.

■ Stabilizer:

Stabilizers fall into three major categories: those that tear away, those that cut away, and those that wash away.

■ *Tear-away:* Use tear-away stabilizers only with woven fabrics. Hoop tear-away with the fabric. Or, use an adhesive spray to adhere the fabric after hooping the stabilizer.

■ *Cut-away:* Cut-away stabilizer is the most versatile. Cut-away stabilizer works for both woven and stretch fabrics. It is essential to use cut-away on knit fabrics. If a tear-away stabilizer is used with knits, it will eventually break down, causing the embroidery stitches to distort with the stretch of the fabric.

■ *Wash-away:* Wash-away's primary purpose is as a topping for napped fabrics to prevent the nap from "peeking through" the embroidery stitches. Wash-away can also be used for embroidering on sheer items such as tulle, organza, or even nylon screening.

- *Water-activated stabilizer:* Use this stabilizer for embroidering bulky items, such as hats and bags, or items that are too small to hoop. Rather than hooping the item to be embroidered, the stabilizer is hooped and the item is temporarily adhered to the stabilizer. Dampening the stabilizer with a sponge activates the adhesive.

- *Temporary spray adhesive:* This can be used to adhere any stabilizer to fabric. It is especially useful when embroidering bulky items because you can spray the stabilizer and use it in the same way you would the water-activated stabilizer.

HOOPING THE FABRIC

While the embroidery machine does much of the work on its own, the end result still relies on the skill of the user. The most difficult step for most embroiderers to learn is hooping. This is the process by which the fabric and stabilizer are placed into the hoop. Use the following basic rules to help improve your hooping technique.

■ Whenever possible, hoop all layers of fabric and stabilizer together. Choose the smallest hoop that will accommodate the design. The fabric should be smooth, not stretched. Keep the fibers "at rest" when in the hoop. If the fabric is stretched in the hoop, the embroidery will hold the stretch in place. Then when the fibers relax out of the hoop, the area around the embroidery will bunch up and create a "bubble."

■ To avoid hoop burn, which creates a shiny, bruised mark where the fabric has been hooped, loosen the screw so that the inner hoop inserts easily into the outer hoop. Once the fabric and inner hoop are halfway into the outer hoop, tighten the screw slightly. Then, push the inner hoop completely into the outer hoop.

The process of tightening the screw slightly once the inner hoop is halfway through reduces the chance of the fabric "bunching" when the outer hoop is too loose. When the inner hoop is pushed into the outer hoop, the fabric stays smooth.

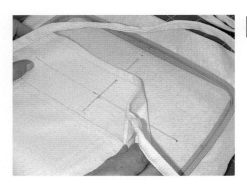

It often helps to rotate the design in order to allow you to hoop the project with the bulk of the fabric toward the outside of the machine. Check your machine's manual for rotating directions.

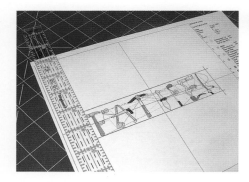

■ After the fabric is in the hoop, tighten the hoop screw to secure the fabric. Using your hands to tighten the screw applies enough pressure to stabilize the fabric. If you tighten with a screwdriver, you risk stripping the screw or the nut.

■ Keep the inner hoop flush with the outer hoop, perhaps even slightly past flush. The fabric should lie flat on the bed of the machine for proper tension between the top thread and bobbin thread.

■ For items that cannot be hooped, use one of the following methods: Hoop the stabilizer. Use temporary spray adhesive to adhere the stabilizer to the item. Or, hoop a piece of water-activated stabilizer, dampen slightly with a sponge, and adhere the fabric to the dampened surface. Let dry momentarily before embroidering. Keep the weight of the project off the hoop, or the weight will pull the hoop. To prevent mishaps, do not leave the machine unattended during embroidery.

■ Print out a paper template of your design using your computer and the *Sew Much Fun* CD software. Use a ruler to draw a box around the design keeping the edges of the box parallel to the horizontal and vertical center markings on the printout of the design.

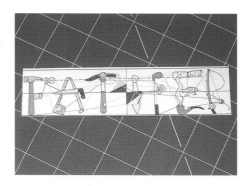

■ Cut out the drawn box. Cut short slits at the intersection of the lines that mark the center of the template. Fold back two opposite corners at the slits for transferring placement lines to the project. Lay out the paper template on the project and determine the placement of the design. Mark the horizontal and vertical axis of each design onto the project.

■ To begin stitching, take the first stitch manually and pull on the top thread to bring the bobbin thread to the top of the fabric. This will keep the bobbin thread tail from bunching up under the design.

■ Many designs will require a change of thread color in the middle of the design. Follow you machine's instruction manual to change threads while you are stitching.

■ Your machine will create beautiful designs only if the thread tension is right. You will need to adjust the tension when you do a test design. The top embroidery thread should be pulled to the back by the bobbin thread so that a line of top thread shows at the edge on the back of the design. Adjust your tension until you obtain this.

■ The easiest way to adjust tension is to embroider the letter "I" and check the tension. If the top thread tension is too tight, it will not show on the back. Also, the bobbin thread will show on the right side of the design (left sample). If the top thread tension is too loose, it will show too much on the back and be somewhat loopy on the front (right sample). The sample in the middle has the proper tension.

■ After sewing the design, remove it from the hoop. Then remove the excess stabilizer and trim the jump stitches, which are the threads that go between the sections of the design as the needle moves from one color section to another section with the same color.

back of design

If using rayon embroidery thread, the upper tension may need to be loosened. Polyester embroidery thread may require a slightly tighter upper tension to avoid looping.

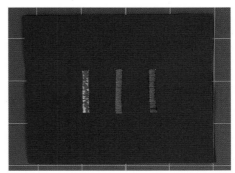

If you are having tension problems, try changing to a new needle or slowing the machine speed.

Remote Control Caddy, page 29

VCR   TV

It's A Good Time To Fish!

Fisherman's Wall Clock, page 13

Vintage Sports Quilt, page 19

Honor
Justice   Freedom
Courage

Snuggle Pillow, page 25

Game Case, page 34

Kay Lynch

FISHERMAN'S WALL CLOCK

- Purchased **fishing hat** with soft brim and crown
- Battery-operated **clock movement** for ¼"-thick clock face, available at most craft shops
- One or more layers **Styrofoam** equal to height of hat crown; project shown requires two layers, each 1¾" thick x approximately 10" square
- One piece of ¼"-thick **cardboard**, approximately 10" square
- Assorted **fishing lures**, optional
- **Embroidery basics:** embroidery thread, bobbin thread, seam sealant, lightweight tear-away stabilizer, temporary spray adhesive, water-soluble or chalk fabric marker, two T-pins, one 1" plastic drapery ring

RC 387 Caddis Dry Fly
For the brim, rotate 90° counter-clockwise. For the 12:00 position on hat crown, mirror the design horizontally.

RC 386 Attractor Dry Fly
For the 3:00 position, mirror the design horizontally and rotate 90° counterclockwise.

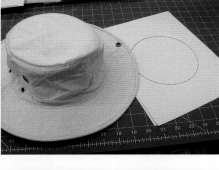

1 To make a pattern for design placement, draw on paper a circle slightly smaller than the top of the hat.

 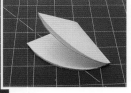

2 Fold the circle in half, then in half again.

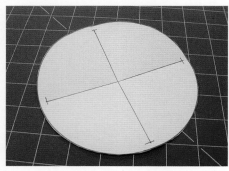

3 Unfold the circle. Draw horizontal and vertical lines along the folds. Mark a point approximately ¼" from the edges of the circle on each line.

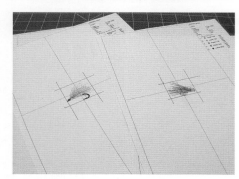

4 Using the CD, print copies of the designs to create templates. Draw a box around each design, keeping the edges of the box parallel to each design's horizontal axis and vertical axis. Cut out the boxes.

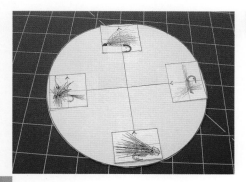

5 Place the boxes on the paper circle. The outside of the design should be near the ¼" marks made in Step 3. Rotate any of the designs for a pleasing arrangement. When you are satisfied with the placement of the designs, tape in place, and cut ¾" to 1" horizontal and vertical slits through the center points of each design and at the circle center.

6 Using a water-soluble marker, mark a horizontal and a vertical line on the top of the hat.

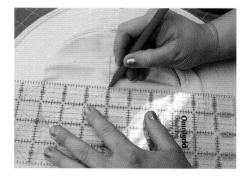

RC 379 Terrestrials Dry Fly

7 Fold back the cut slits, as shown. Place the circle with the designs on the hat top. Transfer the center marks of each design to the hat, using a water-soluble marker. Mark the top of each design with an arrow.

RC 381 March Brown Fly

8 Mark the 12:00 position with a water-soluble marker. Transfer the horizontal and vertical lines to the underside of the hat top to help placement within the hoop.

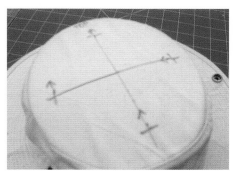

Use your machine's built-in letters or your favorite lettering software to embroider the words for this project. The letters shown are 1" tall.

9 Hoop two layers of lightweight tear-away stabilizer. Mark the center horizontal and vertical lines. Spray the stabilizer with temporary spray adhesive.

10 Scrunch the crown of the hat and smooth sides so the top will lie flat against the stabilizer.

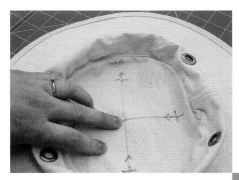

If you hoop's sewing field is 4" or smaller, you will need to match the horizontal and vertical axis of each design with those in the hoop. You will need to re-hoop for each design.

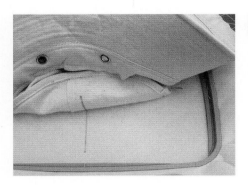

11 Place the hat on top of the sprayed stabilizer, matching the horizontal and vertical axis of the hat with those of the hoop. Smooth the top so that there are no wrinkles and the sides are out of the way.

EMBROIDER THE DESIGNS

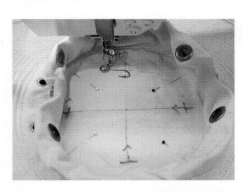

1 For each design, move the needle to the center position of that design. Use your machine's trial or check feature to ensure that the design will stitch properly on the hat top.

2 Embroider designs at the 12:00, 3:00, 6:00, and 9:00 positions.

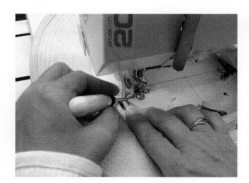

3 Use an awl or other pointed object to hold the excess hat fabric out of the way as the embroidery is being done. It is helpful to slow the machine's speed when you are working in a close area.

4 Plan the placement of the wording around the brim of the hat. Use the "arcing feature" in your embroidery software (refer to the instruction manual) to arc the bottom of the wording to match the arc of the hat brim. Print the letters first for the most accurate placement of the wording. Print a template of the RC 387 and position it on one side of the brim. Rotate the design to fit. Transfer the horizontal and vertical markings of each set of words and the dry fly design to the hat brim. Draw an arrow indicating the top of the wording and the design.

5 Hoop two layers of tear-away stabilizer. Mark the horizontal axis and the vertical axis on the stabilizer. Spray the stabilizer with temporary spray adhesive. Position the horizontal and vertical axis of the top wording on the marked horizontal and vertical axis. (See text at the right.) Embroider the "It's A Good" phrase. Repeat to embroider the bottom words "Time To Fish" and the dry fly design. After the embroidery is finished, remove the stabilizer from the back. Remove any positioning marks from the hat.

The capital letters on the sample are approximately 1" tall and were created in Artista embroidery software program. Each word was created separately with a circular baseline using a radius of approximately 6". This was the radius of this particular hat from the center to about ⅝" from the outside edge of the hat brim. Measure the radius of your hat and position the letters accordingly.

ASSEMBLE THE PROJECT

1 Place the hat upside down on tracing paper and trace the outline of the hat's top. Cut a cardboard circle the exact size. Then, cut the Styrofoam the same size. ("Sand" the rough edges of the Styrofoam with a scrap piece of Styrofoam.) Set aside the Styrofoam until the clock mechanism is ready to be installed. Insert the cardboard into the crown of the hat. It should fit snugly to help keep it taut. Trim the cardboard to fit, then spray lightly with adhesive and re-insert in the hat.

If you do not have an arcing feature, draw an arc on the hat brim and position the letters manually. You may first want to do a test on a circle of fabric cut to the size of the hat brim.

If the hat needs more thickness to hold the clock tightly in place, cut another piece of Styrofoam the same size or slightly larger depending on the shape of the hat. There is no need to cut a hole in this piece as long as you do not glue it in place and cover the clock mechanism permanently, or cut a hole in this piece if you plan to glue it on and cover the clock mechanism permanently.

2 Find the center of the hat's crown. Using an awl, punch a hole the diameter of the clock's center shaft at the hat center, pushing through the cardboard. Apply seam sealant around the hole and allow to dry.

3 Insert the Styrofoam in the crown of the hat. Transfer the center mark to the Styrofoam by punching a hole in the Styrofoam with an awl. Remove the Styrofoam from the hat. Center the clock mechanism on the piece of Styrofoam and trace around it.

4 Cut along the traced lines to make a hole in the Styrofoam. This will hold the clock mechanism in place when it is in the hat. ("Sand" rough edges of the Styrofoam with a scrap piece of Styrofoam.)

5 Assemble the clock face, per the manufacturer's instructions. The top of the hat (with the cardboard as reinforcement) is the "clock face." Once the clock is assembled, install a battery. Spray one side of the Styrofoam with temporary spray adhesive. Position the Styrofoam around the clock mechanism to secure in place.

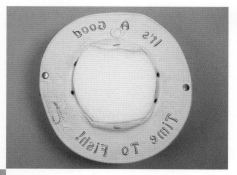

6 On the back, insert T-pins through the hat band and into the Styrofoam to secure the hat to the foam. Sew a drapery ring on the back of the hat brim for hanging. Add optional fishing lures as desired.

CHRISTY BURCHAM
31 ½" x 40"

VINTAGE
SPORTS QUILT

PROJECT **MATERIALS LIST**

- ¾ yard **light flannel** fabric
- ½ yard **medium flannel** fabric
- 2½ yards **dark flannel** fabric (includes backing and binding)
- 34" x 42" piece of **batting**
- **Embroidery basics**: embroidery thread, bobbin thread, lightweight tear-away stabilizer, temporary spray adhesive, water-soluble or chalk fabric marker

SP 957 All Sport

SP 966 Football Player

SP 960 Slugger

Optional Cutting Instructions:

If you are not using checked or plaid fabric and don't want Block A to have bias edges, you can cut the light side and corner triangles as follows: Cut two 4¼"-wide strips, then cut the strip into twelve 4¼" squares. Cut the square diagonally twice to make 48 side triangles. Cut one 2⅜" strip, then cut the strip into twelve 2⅜" squares. Cut the squares in half diagonally to make 24 corner triangles.

1 **Light Flannel:**

Cut one 2⅝"-wide strip, then cut the strip into twelve 2⅝" squares for Block A.

Cut two 3"-wide strips, then cut the strips into twenty-four 3" squares. Cut the squares in half diagonally to make 48 half-square triangles for Block A side triangles.

Cut two 3⅜"-wide strips, then cut the strips into twelve 3⅜" squares. Cut the squares in half twice diagonally for 48 quarter-square triangles for Block A corner triangles.

Cut one 4½"-wide strip, then cut the strip into six 4½" squares for Block B.

2 **Medium Flannel:**

Cut four 2⅝"-wide strips from the medium flannel. Set aside 2 strips. Cut the remaining 2 strips into twenty-four 2⅝" squares for Block A.

Cut four 3½" squares for the border corners.

3 **Dark Flannel:**

Cut two 4⅝"-wide strips from the dark flannel, then cut the strips into twelve 4⅝" squares. Cut the squares in half diagonally to make 24 half-square triangles for Block B.

Cut one 9¾"-wide strip, then cut the strip into three 9¾" squares. Cut the squares in half diagonally twice to make 10 quarter-square triangles for the side setting triangles.

Cut two 5⅛" squares, then cut the squares in half diagonally once to make 4 half-square triangles for the corner setting triangles.

Cut two 3½" x 34½" strips for the side borders.

Cut two 3½" x 26" strips for the top and bottom borders.

ASSEMBLE THE BLOCKS

Use ¼" seam allowance for all seams. Press each seam toward the darker fabric where possible.

1 For Block A, sew the two 2⅝"-wide medium strips to either side of the 2⅝"-wide light strip. Press. Cut into twelve 2⅝"-wide units.

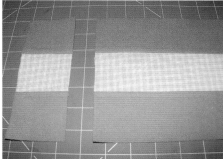

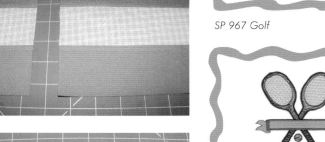

SP 967 Golf

2 Sew a light quarter-square triangle to each end of the unit, matching center points. Press carefully since the edges of the triangles are bias.

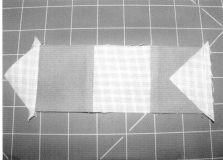

SP 976 Tennis

3 Sew a light half-square triangle to opposite sides of a 2⅝" medium square. Make 2 for each block, 24 total. Press carefully.

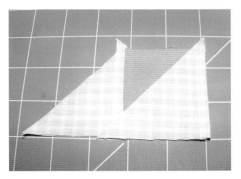

SP 970 LaCrosse

4 Sew a light quarter-square triangle to the top of the unit, matching center points. Make 2 for each block. Press carefully.

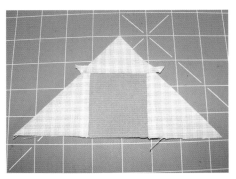

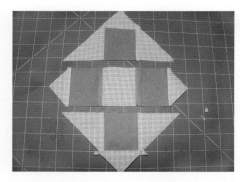

5 Sew a triangle unit onto each side of the center strip, matching seams. Press block carefully since the edges are bias. The blocks should measure 6½" square.

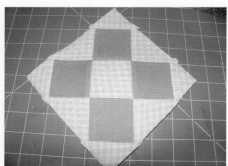

6 Repeat the process to make 12 of Block A.

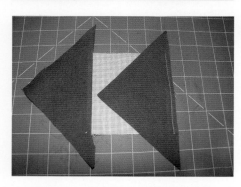

7 For Block B, sew dark half-square triangles to opposite sides of six 4½" light squares, matching center points. Press.

8 Repeat the process for the remaining 2 sides of the square. Make 6 of Block B. Do not trim yet.

1 Mark a horizontal and a vertical line on a piece of lightweight tear-away stabilizer. Layer atop 2 additional pieces of lightweight tear-away stabilizer. Hoop the 3 layers of stabilizer, making sure the marked piece is on top. As you hoop, use the hoop's grid to make sure that the marked lines are centered.

2 Spray the stabilizer with temporary spray adhesive.

3 Adhere one Block B to the stabilizer, aligning the center of the block with the marks on the stabilizer. Note: The block will be on point, but the center light square will be straight.

4 Embroider the desired design. Depending on the size of the design, the embroidery may overlap the seam slightly. This is not a problem and actually adds interest to the quilt. Remove the hoop from machine and gently tear away the stabilizer. Repeat the process for the remaining 5 blocks, each with a different sport.

5 Trim the blocks to 6½" square.

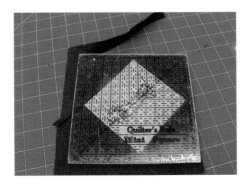

1 Arrange the blocks and setting triangles, as shown.

2 Sew blocks in diagonal rows. Press carefully to avoid stretching the bias edges. Sew the rows together. Press.

3 Sew the 3½" x 34½" dark border strips to each side of the quilt. Press.

4 Sew 2 medium 3½" blocks to each end of the 3½" x 26" border strips. Press.

5 Sew to top and bottom of quilt, matching seams at the corners. Press.

QUILT

1 Place the backing fabric wrong side up on a flat surface. Spray the entire back with temporary spray adhesive. Place the batting over the backing fabric, smoothing the fabric.

2 Spray the batting fabric with temporary spray adhesive. Place the quilt top over the batting, smoothing the fabric.

3 Machine quilt the layers together by stitching in the ditch or by free-motion quilting, as desired.

FINISH

1 Cut four 3"-wide strips of dark flannel and piece end to end, as needed, to make a 150" binding strip. Fold the strip in half lengthwise, with wrong sides together, and press.

2 Using a ½" seam allowance, stitch the binding to top side of the quilt, mitering the corners. Overlap the ends of the binding so the raw edges do not show.

3 Fold the binding to the quilt back and press. Slipstitch the binding in place.

Christy Burcham

SNUGGLE PILLOW

PROJECT **MATERIALS LIST**

- ½ yard lightweight **leather, suede, or synthetic suede**
- 2 yards ½" decorative **cording** to match leather
- 16" **pillow form**
- 18" (or longer) **zipper** to match leather
- **Embroidery basics:** embroidery thread, bobbin thread, cut-away stabilizer, temporary spray adhesive, water-soluble or chalk fabric marker

LJ 131 Freedom Soars

NV 088 Star

1 Cut a 17" square of leather fabric and two 17" squares of cut-away stabilizer.

2 Cut two 9" x 17" rectangles of leather fabric.

EMBROIDER THE DESIGNS

1 Mark the exact center of the 17"-square pillow front. Print designs LJ 131 and NV 088 and position the motifs on the pillow front as desired. Mark the designs' centers and draw an arrow to indicate the top of each design.

2 Spray 2 layers of cut-away stabilizer with temporary spray adhesive. Affix to the back of the pillow fabric under the center mark. Hoop and embroider the center design LJ 131. You may need to rotate the design to fit your hoop. Remove the hoop from the machine and the fabric from the hoop.

3 To keep the hoop from crushing the center design, embroider the remaining designs and lettering with the fabric adhered to hooped stabilizer. Draw a horizontal and a vertical axis on the stabilizer and place the stabilizer in the hoop.

4 Spray the stabilizer with temporary spray adhesive. Align the center points of the design and the stabilizer; press gently to adhere. Place the hoop on the machine and embroider each design. Refer to page 17 for details about placement of the words.

5 Once the embroidery is complete, trim the jump stitches and cut the excess stabilizer from the back of the design. Trim the top to 15½" square. Remove any markings from the front of the pillow.

Use your machine's built-in letters or your favorite lettering software to embroider the words for this project. The letters shown are 1½" tall.

ASSEMBLE THE PILLOW

1 With right sides together, align the zipper tape with the 17" cut edge of one 9" x 17" pillow back.

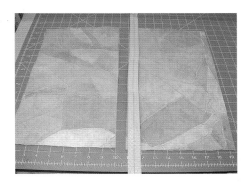

2 Using the zipper foot of your sewing machine, stitch close to the zipper teeth.

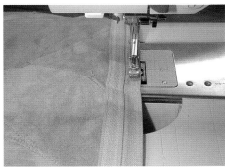

3 Finger-press the fabric back, exposing the zipper teeth.

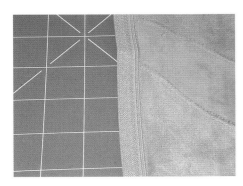

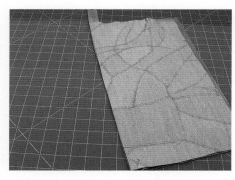

4 Place the pillow back pieces together, with right sides facing. Stitch close to the zipper teeth. Finger-press the fabric back, exposing the zipper.

5 Machine-baste the cording to the front of the pillow slightly rounding the corners, using a ½" seam allowance. Overlap the ends.

6 Place the pillow back right side up. Unzip the zipper about half way.

FINISH

1 Center the pillow top on the pillow back, right sides together. Note: The pillow back will be larger than the pillow front. Do not trim to match at this time.

2 Using a zipper foot and a ½" seam allowance, stitch the top to the back of the pillow all the way around the pillow. Trim the edges and the corners. Turn the pillow right side out through the zipper opening. Insert the pillow form and zip the pillow closed.

MARY GRIFFIN

REMOTE CONTROL CADDY

PROJECT **MATERIALS LIST**

- ¾ yard **denim** or similar weight fabric
- ½ yard **plaid fabric** for piping and lining
- 2½ yards ¼" **cord** for piping or use purchased piping
- 11" x 25" piece of **batting**
- **Embroidery basics**: embroidery thread, bobbin thread, heavy-weight cut-away stabilizer, bobbin thread, temporary spray adhesive, water-soluble or chalk fabric marker

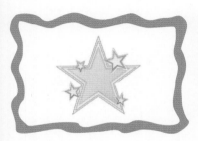

SP 996 "Stars"

1 Cut one 11" x 25" piece of **denim** for the caddy top

2 Cut two 12" x 14" pieces of **denim** for the pockets

3 Cut one 11" x 25" piece of **plaid fabric** for the caddy lining

4 Cut one 11" x 25" piece of **batting**

EMBROIDER THE DESIGNS

Use your machine's built-in letters or your favorite lettering software to embroider the words for this project. The letters shown are 1" tall.

1 Mark the vertical and the horizontal axis at the center of the caddy top, right side up. Spray cut-away stabilizer with temporary spray adhesive; adhere the stabilizer to the wrong side of the denim. Hoop both layers.

2 Embroider the Stars SP 996 in the center.

Centering the Design:
The Star art has several points which may create an optical illusion when centering the design. Remember to use the center of the large star for placement.

3 Mark and stabilize one pocket in the same way as the caddy top. Using your machine's large embroidery hoop and lettering software (or built-in machine lettering), center and embroider the words PROGRAM GUIDE on the first pocket. If your machine's hoop will not accommodate the entire design, embroider part of the letters at a time, then rehoop.

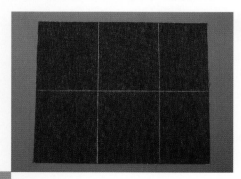

4 To mark the second pocket for embroidery, draw a horizontal line across the center. Then draw a vertical line 4" from the right edge and a second vertical line 5" from the left edge.

5 Using the previously drawn lines as center points, hoop with cut-away stabilizer and embroider TV on the right marking. Re-hoop and embroider VCR on the left marking.

6 Trim the excess stabilizer from the embroidered designs. Trim the pockets to measure 9" high x 11" wide. Turn down the top edges of the pockets ¼" twice and topstitch the hems.

ASSEMBLE THE CADDY

1 Baste the pockets to each end of the caddy, or spray the edges of the pockets with temporary spray adhesive to hold them in place.

2 Mark the center of the remote control pocket and stitch through all layers to divide the pocket.

3 Baste the batting to the wrong side of the caddy, or spray the batting with temporary spray adhesive to hold it in place.

CREATE THE PIPING

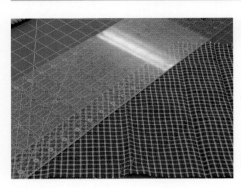

1 Fold the remaining plaid fabric on the bias. Cut at the fold, then cut 1½"-wide strips. Sew the strips together as needed to create a strip at least 80" long.

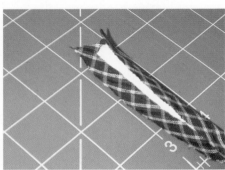

2 Fold the bias strip in half, wrong sides together, and sandwich the purchased cord inside.

3 Starting ½" from the end of the piping, machine-baste close to the piping, using a zipper foot.

1 Baste the finished piping to the right side of the caddy, matching the raw edges.

2 Using a zipper foot, stitch the lining to the caddy, right sides together, leaving an opening for turning. Trim seam allowances.

3 Turn the caddy right side out. Press and slipstitch the opening closed. Remove any markings from the front. Drape the caddy over the arm of a chair and let the sports season begin!

MARY GRIFFIN

GAME CASE

PROJECT **MATERIALS LIST**

- 1¼ yards **poplin**
- 1 yard **hook-and-loop tape**
- **Embroidery basics**: embroidery thread, bobbin thread, heavy-weight cut-away stabilizer, temporary spray adhesive, water-soluble or chalk fabric marker

1 To cut fabric for the **case front**, measure the largest of your folded game boards. Double the folded board width and add 2½". Also add 2½" to the board length. (For the project, the largest board measures 7½" wide x 15" long, folded, so the fabric was cut 17½" x 17½").

2 Cut two pieces of fabric for the **board pockets** using the following formula: Measure the width of the folded board, then add 1½" for the width. For the length, measure the length of the board and add 2½". (For the project, the board measures 7½" wide x 15" long, so the pockets were cut 9" x 17½".)

3 Cut four 9" square pieces of fabric for the two **game-piece pockets**. (Increase the size of the pockets, if needed, to accommodate your game pieces. Allow 1" for the top hems and ½" each for the side and bottom seams.)

4 Cut two 4" x 12" pieces of fabric for the **handles**.

5 Cut two 7" and four 4" lengths of **hook-and-loop tape**.

RC 450 Card & Dice

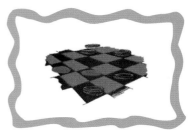

RC 142 Checkers

RC 448 Snake Eyes

Use your machine's built-in letters or your favorite lettering software to embroider the letters for this project. The letters shown are ⅜" tall.

EMBROIDER THE DESIGNS

1 Fold the case front in half, then press and mark the crease. Also mark the center of each side.

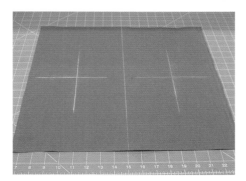

2 Spray cut-away stabilizer with temporary spray adhesive; adhere the stabilizer to the wrong side of the fabric. Hoop both layers.

3 Embroider the checkers design, RC 142, on one half of the case front, using the marked center points.

4 Turn the case front the other direction and embroider the Cards and Dice design, RC 450, on the other side.

5 Mark the centers of the game piece pocket fronts. Spray cut-away stabilizer with temporary spray adhesive; adhere it to the wrong side of the fabric and hoop both layers.

6 Embroider the Snake Eyes design, RC 448, on one pocket front.

7 Use your machine's built-in lettering to create letters for the pocket that holds the Scrabble game pieces.

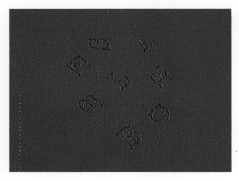

1 Press the top edges under ½" on of all four game-piece pocket sections. Press under ½" again to form the hems. Pin in place.

2 Using temporary spray adhesive, center and adhere the 7" pieces of hook and loop tape over the hem edges. Place the loop side on the front section of each pocket opposite the hook side on the back section.

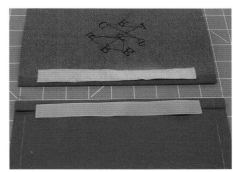

3 Topstitch the hems in place, catching the tape as you sew.

4 Cut four 4" pieces of hook-and-loop tape. Stitch the two loop pieces to the back section of each game-piece pocket 1½" apart.

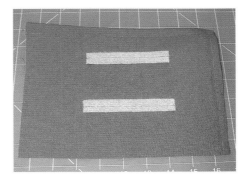

5 With right sides together, sew or serge the game-piece pocket front and back sections together along the side and bottom seams. Turn right side out and press.

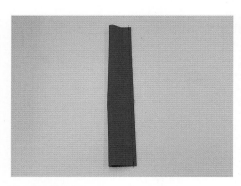

1 Fold the straps in half lengthwise, right sides together. Stitch, using a ¼" seam allowance.

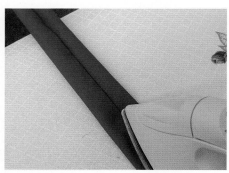

2 Turn and press the seam to the center.

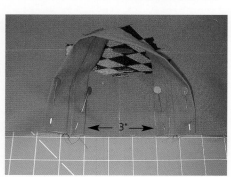

3 With right sides together, center the straps on each side of the case front, leaving 3" between the strap's inner edges. Baste.

1 Lay the game-piece pocket backs on the board pockets to determine the placement of the 4" hook pieces. Pin the hook tape in place. Sew the tape to the board pockets so the game-piece pockets will attach on opposite sides.

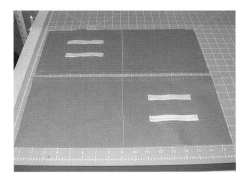

2 Press the top edges under ½" on the board pockets. Press under ½" again to form hems. Topstitch.

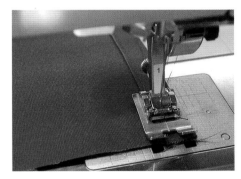

3 With right sides together, pin the board pockets to the case front.

4 Sew or serge the pockets to the front, using a ½" seam allowance.

5 Remove any markings from the front. Turn right side out and press.

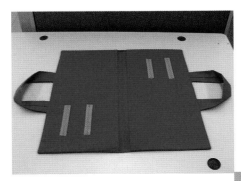

6 Edgestitch the sides of the case.

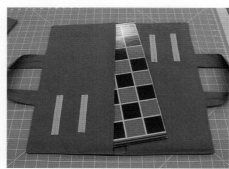

7 Slide the game boards into the case.

8 Put the game pieces into the pockets.

9 Attach the game-piece pockets to the case with the hook-and-loop strips.

10 Fold the case to carry it.

Honey Do Note Holder, page 46

Notes

milk eggs rice

dentist 3 pm

Magnetic Chalkboard, page 42

KITCHEN COMPLEMENTS

MARY GRIFFIN

MAGNETIC CHALKBOARD

PROJECT MATERIALS LIST

- ½ yard **chalkboard fabric**
- 1 yard **complementary solid fabric** for borders and lining
- ⅛ yard **print fabric** for corners
- 15½" square **lightweight batting**
- 11" square **needlepoint canvas**
- 4 round **magnets**
- 2 pieces **chalk**
- **Embroidery basics**: embroidery thread, bobbin thread, monofilament thread, lightweight tear-away stabilizer, temporary spray adhesive, water-soluble or chalk fabric marker, craft glue

PREPARE THE FABRIC

1 Cut one 11½" square of **chalkboard fabric**.

2 Cut one 15¾" square of **solid fabric** for lining. Cut four 8½" x 17" pieces of **solid fabric** for the borders.

3 Cut two 2¾" x 3" pieces of **print fabric** for lower border corners. Cut two 2¾" squares of **print fabric** for upper border corners.

4 Cut twelve 8½" squares of lightweight tear-away stabilizer.

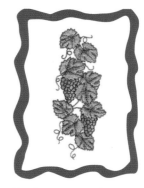

FM 204 Grapevine Border

FM 205 Grapevine Border 2

EMBROIDER THE DESIGNS

1 Spray each stabilizer piece with temporary spray adhesive. Adhere three pieces together to create four stacks. Adhere a stack to the center of each 8½" x 17" piece of solid fabric.

2 To make the side borders, hoop the first solid piece, center and embroider the Grapevine Border design FM 204. Mirror-image the same design and embroider the second solid piece. Embroider the third solid piece with Grapevine Border 2 design, FM 205 for the bottom border.

3 Using built-in lettering on your machine or lettering software, create the word NOTES and embroider this on the fourth solid piece for the top border.

Use your machine's built-in letters or your favorite lettering software to embroider the word for this project. The letters shown are 1¼" tall.

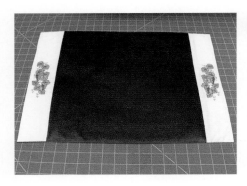

1 Trim the two side grapevine borders to 2¾" x 11½", keeping the design centered. Place these borders on the left and right sides of the chalkboard fabric, so that the grapevines face each other. Sew with right sides together using a ¼" seam allowance. Press.

2 Trim the NOTES border to 2¾" x 11½" and the bottom grapevine border to 2¾" x 16", centering each design.

3 With right sides together and using a ¼" seam allowance, sew the upper border corners to the ends of the NOTES border. Press. With right sides together, sew to the top of the chalkboard fabric, using a ¼" seam allowance. Press.

4 Sew the bottom border to the bottom of the chalkboard, using a ¼" seam allowance. Press.

5 Turn under one 2¾" edge of each lower border corner ¼" twice and topstitch the hem. Place the corners on the lower border, as shown, with ¼" extending beyond the corner of the chalkboard. Stitch ¼" from the edge of the border corner, as shown.

6 Flip the border corners over and baste to the bottom edges of the borders, so that they form pockets. Remove stabilizer from behind all designs.

ASSEMBLE THE NEEDLEPOINT CANVAS

1 Glue magnets to the four corners on one side of the 11" square of needlepoint canvas. Center and glue the 15½" square of batting to the other side of the canvas.

2 Spray the batting side with temporary spray adhesive and adhere it to the wrong side of the chalkboard front.

FINISH

1 Place the chalkboard/canvas/ batting unit on the lining, with right sides together. Using a ¼" seam allowance, sew all edges, leaving a 6" opening for turning.

2 Trim corners, then turn right side out and slipstitch the opening closed. Press. Topstitch ¼" from all edges.

3 Using monofilament thread in the needle, stitch in the ditch through all layers around the chalkboard.

4 Place chalk in a corner pocket.

MARTHA SHERIFF

HONEY DO
NOTE HOLDER

PROJECT MATERIALS LIST

- ¼ yard **denim-weight fabric**
- 9" piece of ¼"-diameter **dowel**
- Small spiral-bound **notepad**
- **Pen** or pencil
- Two ⅞"-diameter **buttons**
- **Twine**, raffia, or jute
- **Embroidery basics**: embroidery thread, bobbin thread, cut-away stabilizer, temporary spray adhesive, water-soluble or chalk fabric marker

PREPARE THE FABRIC

1 Cut two 9" x 12" pieces of denim-weight fabric.

2 Cut a 12" square of stabilizer.

3 Trace and cut a paper pattern using the pattern on page 49.

EMBROIDER THE DESIGN

Honey Do List

1 Using temporary spray adhesive, adhere the cut-away stabilizer to the fabric back. Mark the pattern on the fabric. Mark the placement for the embroidery design on the front using horizontal and vertical lines.

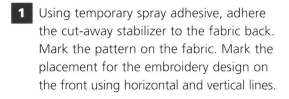
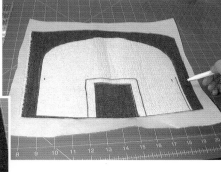

2 Hoop and embroider the design. (Do not remove the stabilizer from the back. It will remain as interfacing in the design.) Remove any marks from the fabric front. Place the embroidered piece on top of another piece of fabric, with wrong sides together, and cut the back and front at the same time.

3 With right sides together, sew the edges, using a ½" seam allowance. Leave a 4" opening on a straight side for turning.

4 Trim seams, clip the curves and corners, then turn right side out. Slipstitch the opening closed. Press. Topstitch around the edges.

5 Make a ½"-long buttonhole ⅜" from the center top to attach a hanger.

6 Fold the flaps 2" to the front, keeping ½" loose at the fold to insert the dowel. Add a button at the center of the flap to secure the fold. Repeat the process for the opposite flap.

FINISH

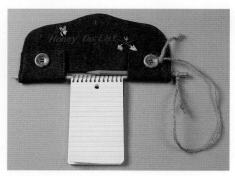

1 Insert the dowel from the outer edge of the holder, through one flap, continuing through the note pad spiral to the opposite flap. Check that the note pad is secure.

2 Tie a pen or pencil to one of the buttons with a piece of twine, raffia, or jute. Hang the holder in a handy place.

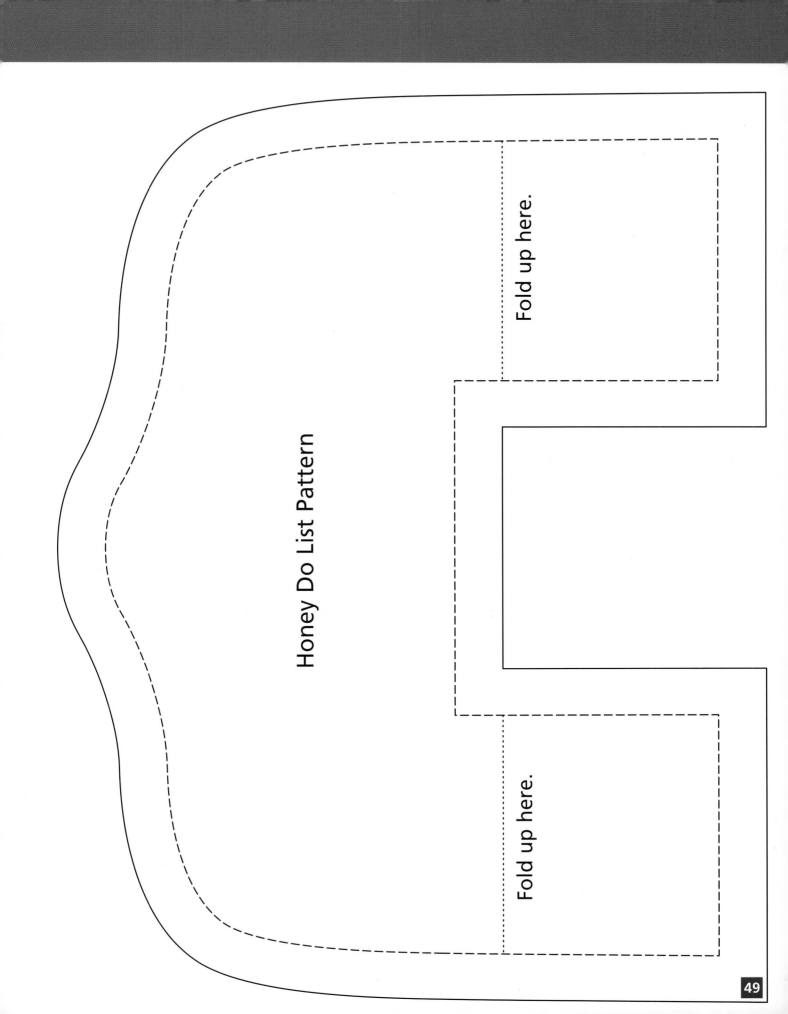

Honey Do List Pattern

Fold up here.

Fold up here.

Flower Pot Stickers, page 51

BEECAUSE I LOVE YOU

Flower Pot Hugger, page 64

Picnic Placemat, page 60

CORN

TOMATO

Garden Quilt, page 55

Christy Burcham

FLOWER POT
STICKERS

PROJECT MATERIALS LIST

- ⅓ yard **nylon organdy** for each sticker

- ⅛"-diameter **wooden dowel** (each stick uses 5½" length of dowel)

- **Embroidery basics:** embroidery thread, bobbin thread, water-soluble stabilizer, temporary spray adhesive, fabric glue, candle or craft heat tool

1 Cut a 10" x 14" piece of nylon organdy.

2 Cut two 10" x 14" pieces of water-soluble stabilizer. Spray one piece of stabilizer with temporary spray adhesive.

If the outer edge of the design is not symmetrical, the second design should be mirror-imaged before embroidering.

EMBROIDER THE DESIGN

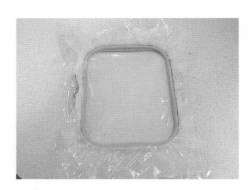

1 Place the organdy on top of the sprayed stabilizer. Spray another piece of stabilizer, and place on top of the organdy. Hoop all layers together, leaving excess fabric at the bottom of the hoop. A second design can be made by rehooping this excess fabric.

NX 757

2 Using the layout function of the machine, move the design to the top of the embroidery hoop. Embroider the design. Rehoop the fabric, making sure there is enough room to embroider another design.

NX 758

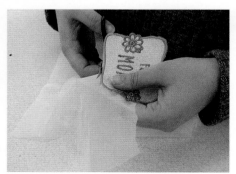

3 Remove the designs from hoop. Trim the threads. Tear away the excess stabilizer. Carefully cut the designs, cutting very close to the design edge. Dissolve any remaining stabilizer.

4 Carefully hold the cut edges of the design over a candle to burn away the excess from the edge. Do not hold the edge too close to the flame or the embroidery thread will also melt. Note: Do not use with a natural fiber thread (rayon or cotton) as danger of fire is increased. Another option is to use a craft heat tool to melt the edges of the design.

NX 763

ASSEMBLE THE FLOWER POT STICKER

1 Coat the back of one design with fabric glue.

NX 768

2 Break or cut the dowel rods into 5½" pieces. Place approximately 2" of dowel rod above the bottom edge of the design.

Personalize your sticker by adding your own lettering. Many types of embroidery software allow you to delete any existing lettering. You may then add your own lettering.

3 Place the other design over the dowel and the first design, matching the edges. Press firmly; let dry.

4 Place the end into a flower pot for a gift or greeting!

KAY LYNCH
51½" x 54"

GARDEN QUILT

PROJECT **MATERIALS LIST**

- 3½ yards green fabric for embroidered bands, backing, and binding
- 1⅝ yards coordinating vegetable print fabric for quilt top
- 56" x 58" piece of batting
- Embroidery basics: embroidery thread, bobbin thread, tear-away stabilizer, temporary spray adhesive, water-soluble or chalk fabric marker

FM 280 Carrot

FM 281 Cauliflower

1 **Green Fabric:**

Cut two 56" lengths. Set aside one of the lengths for the quilt backing.

From the second length, cut two 9" x 56" lengthwise strips for the embroidered bands. Set aside the remaining fabric for the backing and binding.

2 **Printed Fabric:**

Cut two 4½" x 54" lengthwise strips for the bands on each end of the quilt.

Use the remaining fabric to cut a 33" x 54" piece for the center panel of the quilt top.

3 **Tear-Away Stabilizer:**

Cut sixteen 9" squares.

EMBROIDER THE DESIGNS

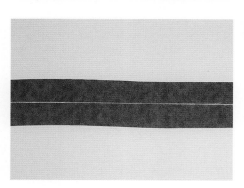

1 On each green 9" x 56" strip, draw a horizontal line along the length of each strip 4½" from both edges. This will be the horizontal center of each of the embroidery motifs.

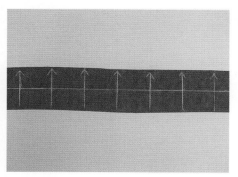

2 Starting 7" from one end, draw 8 vertical lines spaced 6" apart on the horizontal line. The intersections will mark the center point of each design. Draw arrows to indicate the top of the design.

3 Spray a 9" square of stabilizer with temporary spray adhesive. Place the area of the fabric to be embroidered on top of the stabilizer, smoothing the fabric.

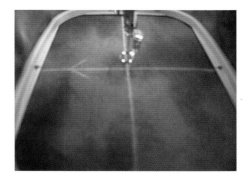

FM 292 Tomato

4 Hoop the fabric and the stabilizer as one, placing the center of the design in the center of the hoop. Attach the hoop to the machine and embroider the design (you may choose to rotate the design for ease in embroidery). Repeat the process for each design. You will make two copies of each design on each band.

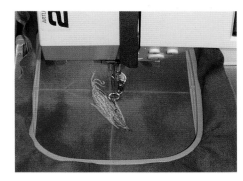

FM 283 Corn

5 Trim each band to 6" x 54", making sure the embroidery designs are centered. Remove any markings

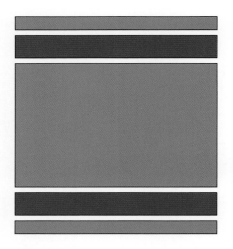

1 With right sides together and using a ¼" seam allowance, sew a green embroidered strip to each long side of the 33" x 54" piece of print fabric. Make sure the top of the designs face the center printed panel. Press.

2 With right sides together and using a ¼" seam allowance, sew a 4½" x 54" strip of print fabric to each end of the blanket top. Press.

ASSEMBLE THE BACKING

1 Cut the large green backing piece in half lengthwise. Trim the smaller piece to 18" x 56". Set aside the remaining fabric for the binding.

2 Using a ¼" seam allowance, sew the three backing pieces together along the long edges, placing the 18" x 56" piece between the two wider pieces. Press. The backing should measure approximately 56" x 58".

QUILT

1 Place the backing fabric wrong side up on a flat surface. Spray the entire back with temporary spray adhesive. Place the batting on the backing fabric, smoothing the fabric.

2 Spray the batting with temporary spray adhesive. Place the quilt top on the batting, right side up, and smooth the fabric.

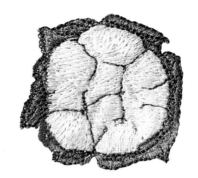

3 Machine-quilt the layers together by stitching horizontal rows 3" apart. Quilt ¼" from the edges of the embroidered bands.

FINISH

1 Cut six 3" strips for the binding and piece together, as needed, to make a 225" strip. Fold the binding strips in half lengthwise, with wrong sides together, and press.

2 Using a ½" seam allowance, stitch the binding to top of quilt, mitering the corners. Overlap the ends of the binding so the raw edges do not show.

3 Fold the binding to the quilt back, and press. Slipstitch the binding in place.

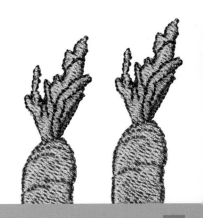

KAY LYNCH

PICNIC
PLACEMAT

- 2⅜ yards **cotton fabric** for placemat fronts and backs
- 1⅛ yards of **polyester fleece**
- 1 yard of **white fabric** for fence pickets
- 4½ yards of **½"-wide elastic**
- **Embroidery basics:** embroidery thread, bobbin thread, temporary spray adhesive, tear-away stabilizer, water-soluble or chalk fabric marker

PREPARE THE FABRIC

1 Cut four 21" x 25" pieces of **cotton fabric** for placemat fronts.

2 Cut four 15" x 20" pieces of **cotton fabric** for placemat backs.

3 Cut forty-four 3" x 9½" rectangles of **white fabric** (11 per placemat) for the pickets.

4 Cut four 15" x 20" pieces of **polyester fleece** for the batting.

5 Cut eight 20" pieces of **elastic** for the fence.

FL 971 Echinacea
Place center point 3" from left side and 4" from the top of the placemat.

FL 974 Flax
Place center point 6" from left side and 5" from the top of the placemat.

FL 983 Rosemary
Place center point 2" from right side and 4" from the top of the placemat.

EMBROIDER THE DESIGNS

1 Draw a rectangle 15" x 20" on each 21" x 25" piece of fabric for the actual placemat size.

2 Print templates of each design. Mark the center point of each design. Using the printouts as templates, position the designs inside the drawn placemat lines (refer to the placement under each design at the right). Keep the edge of the design at least 1" from the drawn lines.

3 Spray a layer of tear-away stabilizer with temporary spray adhesive. Place the area of the fabric to be embroidered on top of the stabilizer, gently smoothing the fabric.

4 Hoop the fabric and the stabilizer as one, placing the center of the design in the center of the hoop. Attach the hoop to the machine and embroider the design. Remove any excess stabilizer from the back of the design. Repeat the process for each design. Remove any markings.

ASSEMBLE THE PICKETS

1 Fold each 3" x 9½" picket strip in half lengthwise, right sides together. Stitch a lengthwise seam using a ¼" seam allowance. Finger-press the seam open and center the seam in the back. Press.

2 Place a dot ½" from the top on the center back seam. Place a dot 1" down on each folded side. Draw a line connecting the dots and stitch along this line. Trim the excess fabric. Turn right side out. Repeat the process for each picket to make 44 total (11 per placemat).

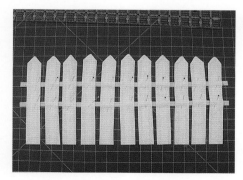

3 To make the fence, place two 20" pieces of elastic 1½" apart. (These will hold the pickets together.) Mark ⅝" from each end of both pieces of elastic. Place the 11 pickets, ½" apart, on top of the elastic, starting and stopping at the ⅝" mark. The tops of the pickets will extend 2½" above the top row of elastic. Pin in place.

4 Sew each picket to the elastic, as shown.

5 Trim the placemat front along the drawn lines, straightening the edges as needed. Place the picket fence, right side up, on the top of the placemat front. Pin the bottom of the pickets along the placemat's lower edge.

6 Machine baste the bottom of the pickets along the lower edge of the placemat. Machine baste the ends of the elastic on the sides of the placemat.

FINISH

1 Place the placemat back and front right sides together. Place a layer of fleece on top. Sew a ½" seam from the edge through all layers, leaving a 6" opening for turning. Trim the corners and turn right side out. Slipstitch the opening closed. Press.

2 To make the napkin and utensil pocket, sew through all layers along the right edge of the fourth picket from the left. Edgestitch around the placemat.

CHRISTY BURCHAM

FLOWER POT HUGGER

PROJECT MATERIALS LIST

- ½ yard of **light-colored fabric**
- 2½ yards of ⅛"-wide coordinating **ribbon**
- **Embroidery basics:** embroidery thread, bobbin thread, heavy-weight cut-away stabilizer, temporary spray adhesive

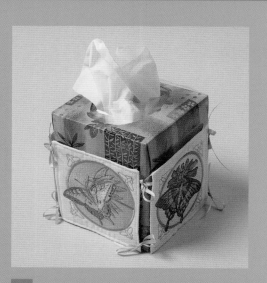

PREPARE THE FABRIC

1 Cut four 9" squares of **fabric**.

2 Cut four 4½" squares of **fabric** for backing.

3 Cut eight 9" squares of heavy-weight cut-away **stabilizer**.

4 Cut sixteen 5" lengths of **ribbon**.

FM 149 Red Spotted Purple

EMBROIDER THE DESIGNS

1 Hoop a 9" square of fabric with two layers of stabilizer. Embroider the first design. Trim threads and remove from the hoop. Press. Do not cut the stabilizer yet.

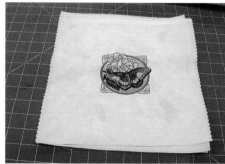

FM 160 Western White

2 Repeat the process for the remaining designs. (You may either repeat the same motif or use different but coordinating designs.)

FM 157 Emerald Swallowtail

ASSEMBLE THE SIDES

1 Trim the embroidered fabric to a 4½" square, centering the embroidery within the square.

FM 155 Swallowtail: Project uses the mirror-imaged design.

2 Flip the square over and mark a line ¼" from the outer edges of the stabilizer.

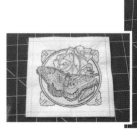
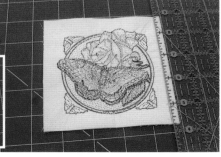

3 Cut the stabilizer only along the marked lines. Wrap the fabric over the edges of the stabilizer. Miter the corners if desired. Press.

4 Mark and fold each side of the backing squares ⅜" under. Miter the corners if desired. Press. The backing square will be slightly smaller than the embroidered square.

5 Spray the back of the embroidered square with temporary spray adhesive. Adhere four pieces of ribbon ½" from the top and bottom edges of each square, with the ribbon ends overlapping the square 1".

6 Spray the wrong side of the backing squares with temporary spray adhesive.

7 Carefully position a backing square over an embroidered square, wrong sides together. Make sure the ribbons are between the two layers and the backing square is centered. Press.

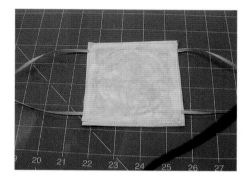

8 Working from the back, stitch along the edge of the backing fabric.

9 Repeat the process for each embroidered square.

FINISH

1 Place two squares side by side. Tie the ribbons and make the bow as desired. Trim the excess ribbon, as needed.

2 Repeat the process until the four squares are tied together to form a box.

Shop Apron, page 72

Nail Bag Apron, page 75

Detail Utility Pail, page 69

KAY LYNCH

DETAIL UTILITY PAIL

PROJECT MATERIALS LIST

- ⅝ yard of 100% polyester mildew-resistant outdoor **canvas** or other heavy-weight fabric
- 1 yard of ⅜"-wide **elastic**
- 2"-thick **foam rubber** (for finished 12" circle)
- 12"-diameter **tabletop wood circle**
- Serrated or electric **knife**
- Four 2" pieces of 1" x 3" **board**
- 3½ gallon or 5 gallon **utility pail**
- 1¼"-long #6 flat-head Phillips wood **screws**
- Wood **glue** and **permanent spray adhesive**
- **Embroidery basics**: embroidery thread, bobbin thread, lightweight tear-away stabilizer, water-soluble or chalk fabric marker

LT 723 '32 Ford Coupe

Use your machine's built-in letters or your favorite lettering software to embroider the words for this project. The letters shown are 1" tall.

1 Trace the 12" wood circle onto the foam. Cut the foam circle using a serrated or electric knife.

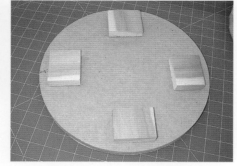

2 Measure the inside diameter of the top rim of the utility pail. Place the wood blocks near the edges of the wood circle, making sure the outer edges of the wood blocks will fit within the rim of the pail. The blocks sit inside the top of the pail to keep the seat from moving around (the project blocks were placed ¾" from the outside of the wood circle).

3 Use glue to set the blocks in place. Secure each block to the tabletop with two wood screws (pre-drilling pilot holes will make inserting the screws easier).

4 Spray the top of the tabletop with permanent spray adhesive. Place the foam circle on top and let dry.

EMBROIDER THE DESIGN

1 Cut a 20" square from the canvas fabric. Fold the canvas in half lengthwise and crosswise. Finger-press the folds and mark. Draw a 10" circle using the intersection of the folds as the center point.

2 Hoop the fabric and stabilizer as one. Embroider the car design in the center of the 20" square. Plan the placement for the wording using the 10" circle as a guide. Use the arcing feature in your embroidery software (refer to the instruction manual) to arc the bottom of the wording to match the circle. Refer to page 17 for further information about placing the letters.

The lettering on the sample is approximately 1" high and was created in Artista embroidery software program. Each word was created separately using a circular baseline with a diameter of approximately 10".

3 Position the word printouts, and transfer the horizontal and vertical axis of the wording to the canvas. Draw arrows to indicate the top of the words.

4 Embroider the words at the top and bottom of the circle. Draw a 19" circle on the fabric centering the embroidery designs. Cut the circle.

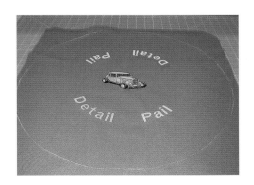

FINISH

1 Select a multiple-step zigzag stitch or a standard zigzag stitch on your conventional sewing machine. Increase the stitch width to approximately 4mm. Place the elastic on the wrong side of the canvas along the cut edge. To start, sew at least 1" without stretching the elastic.

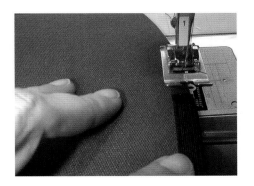

2 Continue sewing the elastic around the entire circle, stretching the elastic as tightly as possible in front of the needle. Place the cover over the foam, wrapping the elastic edge under the seat.

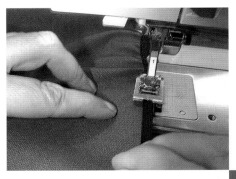

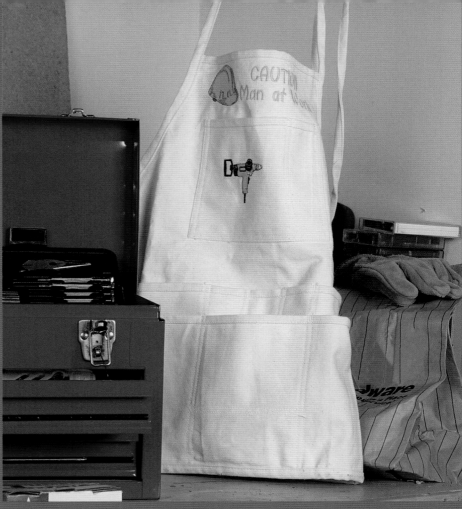

Kay Lynch

SHOP APRON

- Purchased **shop apron**
- **Embroidery basics:** embroidery thread, bobbin thread, tear-away stabilizer, temporary spray adhesive, water-soluble or chalk marker

PREPARE THE FABRIC

1 To determine design placement at the top, fold the apron in half and mark the center. Align the vertical center of the design with this mark, and adjust it up or down, as needed. Draw a horizontal line parallel to the top of the apron.

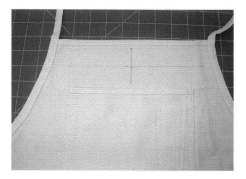

LH 815 D-Handled Drill

EMBROIDER THE DESIGN

1 Hoop 2 layers of tear-away stabilizer. Draw a horizontal and vertical line through the center of the hoop on the stabilizer. Spray the stabilizer with temporary spray adhesive. Place the apron on the sprayed stabilizer. Smooth the area to be embroidered. Embroider the design.

LH 893 Hard Hat

2 Print a template of each design, and plan the design placement on the pocket. Place the paper template on the pocket in the desired position and mark the center horizontal and vertical crossmarks on the apron. Extend the length of the cross marks several inches.

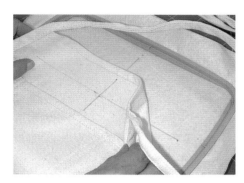

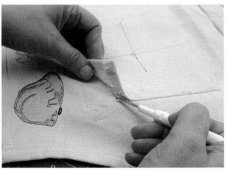

Use your machine's built-in letters or your favorite lettering software to embroider the words for this project. The letters shown are ¾" tall.

3 Some stitching will have to be removed from the apron before you can embroider the pocket. Sometimes you can remove the stitching on just the two sides and leave the bottom of the pocket stitched to the garment. The pocket on the sample has additional stitching for pencils and small tools, so the left side and bottom stitching was removed.

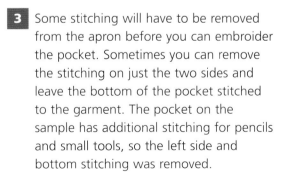

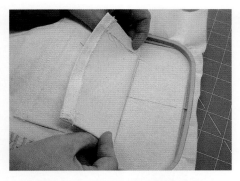

4 Hoop 2 layers of tear-away stabilizer. Draw a horizontal and vertical line through the center of the hoop on the stabilizer. Align the cross marks on the apron pocket with the cross marks on the hooped stabilizer. Place the bulk of the fabric on the side of the hoop that will be to the left of the needle when it is placed on the machine.

5 Carefully fold excess apron fabric out of the way of the hoop. You may need to rotate the design to face toward the top of the apron.

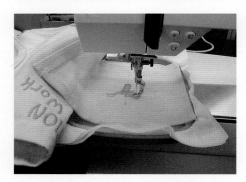

6 Embroider the design, making sure to monitor the embroidery at all times. Ensure the apron does not get caught accidentally in the stitching, and the extra fabric does not interfere with the movement of the hoop.

FINISH

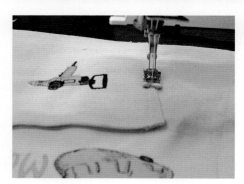

1 Remove the design from the hoop. Remove the stabilizer from the back and trim the threads, then re-sew the pocket into place. Remove any markings.

Kay Lynch

NAIL
BAG APRON

PROJECT MATERIALS LIST

- Purchased **nail bag apron**
- **Embroidery basics**: embroidery thread, bobbin thread, tear-away stabilizer, water-soluble or chalk fabric marker, temporary spray adhesive

LH 838 Father

LH 804 Pipe Cutter

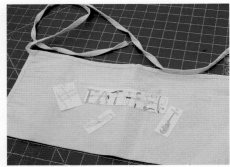

1 Print out the templates for each design. Lay the paper templates on the apron to determine the placement of the motifs. Measure the distance on each end of "Father" to ensure that the design is centered.

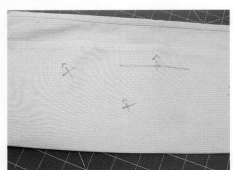

2 Place the templates for the other tools randomly on the apron. Mark a horizontal and a vertical axis of all the designs. Draw arrows to denote the top of the design.

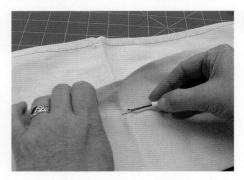

3 If you are embroidering on pockets, it will be necessary to remove stitching from the apron so that you can hoop the stabilizer and then adhere the pocket to the stabilizer.

EMBROIDER THE DESIGNS

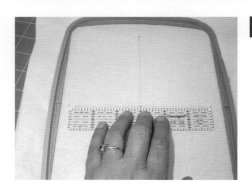

1 Hoop two or three layers of tear-away stabilizer. Mark a horizontal and a vertical axis on the stabilizer.

2 Spray the stabilizer in the hoop with temporary spray adhesive. Align a horizontal and a vertical axis of the apron with the marks on the stabilizer. Allow most of the excess to be to the left of the machine needle when the hoop is placed on the machine. Smooth the area to be embroidered. Carefully fold any excess apron fabric out of the way of the hoop.

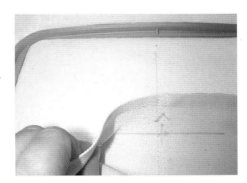

3 Attach the hoop to the machine. Embroider the design. Monitor the embroidery at all times to ensure that the apron does not accidentally get caught in the stitching and to make sure that the extra fabric does not interfere with the movement of the hoop.

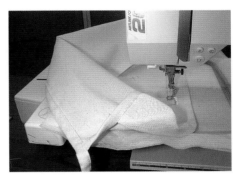

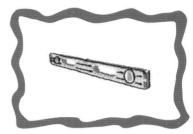

LH 803 Framing Level

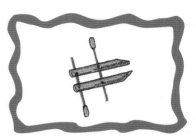

LH 807 "J" Handscrews

FINISH

1 Remove the embroidery hoop from the machine. Remove the design from the hoop, then remove any excess stabilizer from the wrong side. Trim threads. Re-sew any pocket seams you removed before embroidery. Remove any markings.

From left to right: Martha Sheriff, Kay Lynch, Christy Burcham, Mary Griffin

Christy Burcham's fascination with sewing began as a child watching her mother (Kay Lynch, co-author of this book) create everything from pageant dresses to pillows in her sewing room. Christy began her own sewing career while still in high school after taking a part-time job at a local sewing machine dealer. Her interest in sewing and embroidery grew as she took classes with local teachers and learned more about various embellishment techniques. Now an educator for Oklahoma Embroidery Supply and Design, Christy writes for *Creative Machine Embroidery* and *Sew News*. She teaches at national shows, including Houston Quilt Market and the Creative Embroidery Conference.

Mary Griffin has 13 years experience in the sewing industry. After serving as an educational consultant for a major sewing machine manufacturer, she recently joined Oklahoma Embroidery Supply and Design as Education Manager. She works with a team responsible for giving dealers and consumers the skills to create professional embroidery on all brands of home embroidery machines. Mary holds a master's degree in textiles from Ohio State University. She conducts national seminars on embroidery and digitizing, is co-author of *Serger Secrets,* and writes for a variety of sewing and embroidery publications.

Kay Lynch began sewing as a young girl, and operated a home-based business doing custom sewing and free-motion embroidery work. She received a Bachelor of Science degree in home economics from Oklahoma State University. She is currently Card Production Assistant at Oklahoma Embroidery Supply and Design. In addition to assisting in the production of embroidery cards, she also develops ideas and makes projects using the designs, and writes articles for publications such as *Creative Machine Embroidery, McCall's Pattern Magazine,* and *Embroidery Journal.* work. She has taught adult serger classes for Canadian Valley Technology Center and at Bernina of Oklahoma City South, and also teaches special classes and seminars throughout Oklahoma City.

Martha Sheriff has been around sewing most of her life, and learned free-motion embroidery in the 70's. Her sister's purchase of an embroidery machine became the perfect opportunity to go into business: that business is now Oklahoma Embroidery Supply and Design. For many years, Martha ran the embroidery machines, and then supervised the production line. She also digitized many of the designs in OESD's catalog and provided training for new embroidery operations. Her sensible, down-to-earth approach to embroidery is considered a great asset by her many successful students.

INDEX

For more information write for a free catalog:

C&T Publishing, Inc.
P.O. Box 1456
Lafayette, CA 94549
(800) 284-1114
e-mail: ctinfo@ctpub.com
website: www.ctpub.com

For quilting supplies:

Cotton Patch Mail Order
3405 Hall Lane, Dept. CTB
Lafayette, CA 94549
(800) 835-4418
(925) 283-7883
e-mail: quiltusa@yahoo.com
website: www.quiltusa.com

Note: Fabrics used in the projects shown may not be currently available since fabric manufacturers keep most fabrics in print for only a short time.

Insert the CD into your PC. The image below will automatically come up on the screen. Click on the option you would like:

Click on the X and you will go back to the opening screen or exit the program when you are in the opening screen.

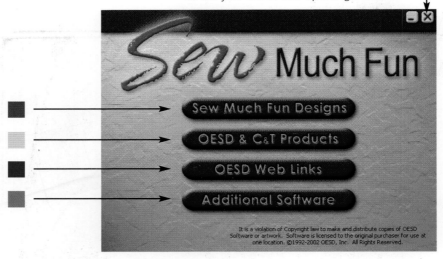

Sew Much Fun Designs:
Sew Much Fun Embroidery Designs: file directory for the embroidery designs. Select the design and the format for your sewing machine and copy it to your computer's hard drive. Transfer the designs to your embroidery machine following the instructions for your embroidery software. Available formats: ART, DST, HUS, JEF, PCS, PES, SEW.

View Sewing Information: View the designs in color. See the design dimensions, number of stitches used, and thread colors for each design.

OESD and C & T Products:
View the product catalogs of Oklahoma Embroidery Supply and Design and C & T Publishing.

OESD Web Links:
Quick link to Oklahoma Embroidery Supply and Design's web site.

Additional Software:
Magician Sizing by Simon and Acrobat Reader (use this option to install Acrobat Reader if it is not already installed on your computer).

For technical support, contact Oklahoma Embroidery Supply and Design at 888-223-6943.

To print a design template using the Magician Sizing Software:
Click on the **File** Menu.

Click on **Print Preview**.

Click on **Options**. In the pop-up menu that appears, choose the **Actual Size** option button and uncheck **Artistic View**.

Click **OK**.

Click **Print**.